SHARON AND BILLY

Alan Bowne

BROADWAY PLAY PUBLISHING INC
224 E 62nd St, NY, NY 10065
www.broadwayplaypub.com
info@broadwayplaypub.com

SHARON AND BILLY
© Copyright 1997 by Alan Bowne

First published by B P P I in *Plays By Alan Bowne* in December 1997
First printing, this edition: February 2014
I S B N: 978-0-88145-593-9

Book design: Marie Donovan
Page make-up: Adobe Indesign
Typeface: Palatino
Printed and bound in the U S A

PLAYS

THE BEANY AND CECIL SHOW

BEIRUT*

FORTY-DEUCE*

SHARON AND BILLY*

*published by Broadway Play Publishing Inc

SHARON AND BILLY was first produced by the Manhattan Class Company (Robert LuPone and Bernard Telsey, Executive Directors), opening on 14 October 1988. The cast and creative contributors were:

MOM ....Sonja Lanzener
DAD ....Richard Grusin
SHARON .... Marisa Tomei
BILLY ....Mathew Vipond

Director .... W D Cantler
Set design ....Gregory Mercurio
Lighting design ....John Hastings
Costume design ....Sam Fleming
Sound design...John Wise
Production manager ....Laura Kravets
Casting ....Laurel Smith
Stage manager................................. Lori Culhane
Co-producer .... Maggie Lear
Associate producer ....Rona Carr

CHARACTERS & SETTING

MOM, *in her thirties*
DAD, *in his forties*
SHARON, *fifteen, aging to seventeen*
BILLY, *thirteen, aging to fifteen*

Time: The late 1950s
The time span covered is nearly two years.

Setting: A single set. The dining room of a blue-collar tract home in a suburb of Los Angeles. Beige walls, chartreuse full-length drapes. Portrait in flocked velvet of a Mexican peasant on one wall. Dining-room table, chairs, and cabinet in the debased "Danish modern" of the period. Door to kitchen, off right; doorway to front room, off left. Across back wall, when drapes drawn, a sliding plate glass door through which is visible a sterile backyard patio and a wretched evergreen elm. The dining room is dominated by the dinner table.

Scenes

Scene One: Dinnertime
Scene Two: Late afternoon, a month later
Scene Three: Dinnertime, three months later
Scene Four: Saturday afternoon, six months later
Scene Five: Evening, six months later
Scene Six: Dinnertime, three months later
Scene Seven: Morning, two weeks later

A Note On The Music:

Some very evocative R & B of the 1950s is used to bridge the scenes of this play. Their placement is specific. Only the first eight to fifteen bars of each song need be played. The songs are as follows:

Opening: *Sincerely* by the Moonglows (Chess, 1581)
1-2: *Sh-Boom* by the Chords (Cat, 104)
2-3: *Sorry (I Ran All the Way Home)* by the Impalas (Cub, 9022)
3-4: *Little Star* by the Elegants (Apt, 2500)
4-5: *Love Is Strange* by Mickey & Sylvia (Groove)
5-6: *Daddy's Home* by Shep & the Limelights (Hull, 740)
6-7: *Come On, Let's Go* by Richie Valens (Marna)
Closing: *Speedo* by the Cadillacs (Josie, 785)

Scene One

(A darkened stage)

(Sound track: Sincerely *by the Moonglows)*

(Music fades. Lights up on:)

(Dinnertime. Drapes open. SHARON, *setting table, to* MOM, *in kitchen, off)*

SHARON: *(Frustrated)* Oh, mother.

MOM: What now?

SHARON: I need a fork.

MOM: Ignatz.

SHARON: And a knife.

*(*MOM *enters; as she hands* SHARON *a fork:)*

MOM: Your father won't like it, it's meat loaf.

SHARON: Never mind.

MOM: What?

SHARON: I needed a *butter* knife.

MOM: I just don't know. *(She exits into the kitchen.)*

SHARON: Oh, mother.

MOM: It's the best I can do, I put onions.

SHARON: Could you bring a spoon?

MOM: Eighty cents a pound for steak. Jeesh.

SHARON: Mother?

(Reenter MOM *with glasses and a butter knife.)*

MOM: Or creamed tuna. Your father won't eat creamed tuna.

SHARON: *(Taking butter knife)* Mother, you won't forget?

MOM: It's too easy to fix, that's why.

SHARON: *(Sarcastic)* Billy likes creamed tuna.

MOM: That's *all* he likes.

(Exit MOM *into kitchen.)*

SHARON: Oh, mother.

MOM: Ignatz.

SHARON: I need *another* spoon. *(She exits into kitchen; as she does so:)* Mother, you won't forget to ask Daddy?

MOM: *(Ignoring her; fussing)* Jeesh.

(Enter BILLY *from front room, left. He sits at table.)*

BILLY: Mom?

MOM: Hmmmm?

(Reenter SHARON, *with spoon and plates.)*

BILLY: What's for dinner?

SHARON: *(Hissing)* Slugs.

MOM: Meat loaf.

BILLY: *(To* SHARON*)* Shut up. *(To himself)* I hate meat loaf.

SHARON: *(Mimics him)* "I hate meat loaf."

BILLY: *(Staring at plate)* This ain't my plate. Mine got dividers!

SHARON: *(Exasperated)* Sorry. *(Calling to* MOM; *singsong)* Mother? I forgot Billy's special plate so his peas don't get mixed in with his mashed po-taaa-toes!

BILLY: Shut up.

MOM: Sharon? Go wake up your father and turn off the T V.

SHARON: Billy, go wake Daddy up.

BILLY: I think he's dead.

SHARON: Dead men don't snore.

BILLY: It's the vibrating chair.

SHARON: Mother, you won't forget?

MOM: *(To sound of spoon against rim of pan)* Go wake your father up. Jeesh. I hate to cook.

BILLY: He died and no one will notice. He'll rot in the vibrating chair, his mouth open like this, and we'll all think he's snoring. But he's dead.

SHARON: Good. Then I can go to the sock hop.

BILLY: At Skate-O-Rama? All those hoods?

SHARON: *(Sarcastic)* No, not at Skate-O-Rama. *(Grins)* Maybe I'll go to Memphis!

BILLY: Where?

SHARON: Where Elvis lives, dummie! *(Shimmies shoulders, sings first verse of "Heartbreak Hotel")*

BILLY: *(Watching her; eagerly)* We could drive there. When I get my car.

SHARON: *(Giggling)* A Billymobile,

BILLY: I'm gonna paint these brodie flames. All over it!

SHARON: *(Snapping fingers)* Yeah!

BILLY: It'll be the cherriest car in Memphis!

SHARON: *(Shimmies)* They got pink Cadillacs!

BILLY: We could burn rubber! All the way to Memphis!

SHARON: They got sock hops every night!

BILLY: Just you and me. Peelin' out! *(He makes motor noises.)*

SHARON: I could have Elvis's baby!

BILLY: And never come back!

(BILLY *and* SHARON *laugh.*)

(*Abruptly,* SHARON *stops laughing, resumes setting table.*)

SHARON: You're not invited. Elvis don't like brains.

BILLY: Oh yeah? So poop on your sock hops. I know where you're going. (*Mimics radio announcer; contemptuously*) "Be there or be square".

SHARON: *You're* square.

BILLY: (*Same*) "All your old girlfriends'll be there, all your old boyfriends'll be there. Every greasy low-rider, every—"

(SHARON *jabs* BILLY's *shoulder sharply with her knuckle.*)

SHARON: Be quiet!

BILLY: Ouch! (*Lower*) "El! Monte! Legion! Staaa-dium!"

SHARON: Billy! He'll hear you.

BILLY: Dad don't even like it when you watch Johnny Otis.

SHARON: Johnny Otis is cool!

BILLY: (*Mimics* DAD) "Nigger music."

SHARON: R 'n B is cool, so shut up.

BILLY: What'll you gimme?

SHARON: (*Arch*) Reefer.

BILLY: (*Shocked*) Huh?

SHARON: Stupid.

(*Enter* MOM *with meat loaf.*)

MOM: Where's your father?

BILLY: I'll get him, Mom.

(*Exit* BILLY, *left.*)

(MOM *begins slicing meat loaf onto plates that* SHARON *passes her.*)

MOM: *(Pausing)* It's awful. I put all these onions in.

SHARON: *(Sarcastic)* Daddy loves onions.

MOM: *(Resuming)* It tastes like onions. I don't care what he says! Go get Billy's plate.

SHARON: *(Into kitchen)* When'll you ask him?

MOM: *(Calling after her)* Don't make a federal case.

(Enter DAD *and* BILLY.)

(Enter SHARON *with* BILLY's *plate.)*

MOM: *(To* DAD, *hastily)* Sharon wants to go out tonight. A dance.

DAD: No.

(All sit.)

(They pass food around and eat in silence.)

DAD: *(To his wife)* It's good, sweetie.

MOM: About two pounds of onions.

BILLY: *(Picking at food)* I hate onions. *(Beat; to his mother, sarcastically:)* Sweetie.

DAD: *(To* BILLY) Eat.

SHARON: *(Tearing into her meal)* It's a sock hop. Brenda's going. And Cheryl.

DAD: *(To* SHARON; *through his food)* Don't get on your high horse.

SHARON: But, Daddy.

DAD: You been out.

SHARON: Yeah, but—

DAD: *(Mimics her)* "Yeahbut. Yeahbut." Don't yeahbut me. *(Eats)* Every Friday and Saturday night for umpteen weeks. *(Chuckles)* You'll wear holes in your socks all these sock hops.

SHARON: Oh, Daddy.

DAD: You're always goin' off someplace! Remember we usta go drivin' in my pickup? Me and my girl and I'd show you stuff. Drove you everywhere.

BILLY: Watts is all I got.

MOM: *(Warning)* Billy.

BILLY: All I got was you'd drive around Watts and yell about the Negroes.

DAD: That's cause you was always such a pill! All you did was complain about the dirt in my pickup! *(Pokes food in mouth; to SHARON)* But you, I'd show you all the places we was puttin' in pipelines. You usta like that. So stay home for once. *(Sentimental)* With your pore old man.

SHARON: *(Under breath)* Shit.

DAD: What did you say?

MOM: The potatoes, honey, they're au gratin, did—

(DAD slams knife and fork on table, rattling the dishes; SHARON recoils.)

MOM: —you notice?

(DAD stares at SHARON, who cowers. Silence. He resumes eating.)

(BILLY surreptitiously pinches SHARON under table as:)

DAD: Listenin' to monkey music and gallavantin' around. Fifteen years old and what? Slings her hips all these petticoats, and now these see-through blouses!

BILLY: *(Plucking at his chest)* Peek-a-boo.

DAD: *(To* BILLY*)* Shut up. *(To* MOM; *indicating* SHARON *with fork)* She can't get into stewardess school lookin' like that!

BILLY: *(Snickering)* Stewardess.

MOM: I know, honey.

DAD: *(Pointing at* SHARON*)* This is not! American Airlines over here!

MOM: No, dear.

BILLY: *I'm* gonna be a rich and famous artist!

MOM: Or a teacher.

DAD: *(Same)* This! Is a Greyhound Bus to Tijuana, is what this is!

MOM: Oh, now.

BILLY: Big old pictures, Dad, a mile long!

DAD: *(To* BILLY*)* Yeah, on the walls of a nuthouse somewhere! *(To* SHARON*)* Breasts like you got shouldn't be on display. *(Points with fork)* This is like. A cellophane package! Of boobs.

MOM: Honey.

SHARON: All the girls wear these!

DAD: All the girls don't got boobs like you! You walk around like that, you're askin' for it. You could get hurt or somethin'.

BILLY: Why?

(Beat)

DAD: *(Staring at his son)* What?

BILLY: If you like a girl's boobs, why would you hurt 'em?

MOM: Stop saying "boobs."

DAD: *(Pointing at* BILLY's *plate)* This here is your special plate, right?

BILLY: Yeah?

DAD: So eat out of it! *(Eating. To* MOM*)* When I was a kid? Back in Chicago? If I saw some girl in this here? I'd'a reached for those things and played basketball with 'em.

BILLY: *Basketball?*

DAD: *(Ignoring this; to* MOM*)* It's a provocation, these soft things like this bouncin' around in public. I wouldn't blame some kid if he—

(Suddenly, DAD *playfully reaches out for* SHARON*; she recoils.)*

SHARON: Daddy!

MOM: Honey, stop it!

DAD: *(Withdrawing hand; laughing)* Well, she's askin' for it!

BILLY: *(Poking* SHARON *under table)* Basketball!

MOM: Honey, we should at least let her throw a party. A few kids—

DAD: What? In *my* house? A buncha hoods? Laying around *my* house?

MOM: A few of the nicer kids, honey—

DAD: You know what you're sayin'? The way boys are today? You want 'em swaggerin' around here actin' like animals? Fulla acne and with switchblades?

MOM: Now, they don't have switchblades.

DAD: Drippin' hair grease all over our rugs?

MOM: It's the *style*, honey.

BILLY: Yeah, like Dennis.

SHARON: *(Kicking* BILLY *under table)* Shut up.

DAD: I can't even look at 'em when they come by to pick her up. (*Jabs fork in* SHARON's *direction*) And she wants to stay out past eleven.

SHARON: Cheryl gets to stay out past midnight.

DAD: At midnight those greaseballs turn into werewolves! I should make it ten.

SHARON: Daddy!

MOM: But if we let her have a party, we'd be here to supervise. They could stay later and have games and—

(DAD *jabs fork into piece of meat. Lifts it*)

DAD: Who put this here?

(MOM *shakes her head.*)

DAD: (*Pointing about him with impaled meat*) Who put the T V out there? Who put clothes on these kids? Who put the money in your hand for those green drapes?

MOM: Chartreuse, honey.

DAD: *Who did that?*

MOM: I know.

(DAD *drops meat on plate.*)

DAD: No hoody dirtheads gonna party in here and put their greasy hands on stuff I worked hard for.

SHARON: (*Under breath*) Wouldn't hurt your old stuff.

DAD: (*To* SHARON) What's your old man do?

(*No response*)

DAD: What does he do all day?

SHARON: It's the biggest sock hop of the year!

DAD: Construction! I'm a foreman in that hot sun, and I got skin problems! We just put in. Fifty inch. A fifty-inch pipeline in Laguna Beach. While you! Are runnin' around niggered up with all this— (*Mimics Chuck Berry*

style guitar, grotesquely) —TWANG-A-BWANG-A-
THUMP-A-THUMP—

(BILLY *joins in under this.*)

BILLY: Rang. A dang. A rang—

MOM: *(Quickly)* Harry Belafonte!

(Abrupt silence, as DAD *stares at* MOM*)*

MOM: She likes Harry Belafonte too, honey.

DAD: *(Nodding ominously)* Oh. *(Beat)* She does? *(He leans forward.)* And because why? *(No response)* She thinks he's. *Cute.*

SHARON: *(Low tones)* He is cute.

DAD: Negroes. Ain't. Cute. You can say they're decent-lookin' sometimes. But never *cute.*

SHARON: What's the difference?

DAD: There's a difference! Cute is like you wanna kiss him. *(Eats)* You wanna kiss those big lips?

SHARON: Can I be excused?

DAD: Finish your dinner.

SHARON: I'm not hungry.

BILLY: *(Aside to* DAD; *setting him straight)* Harry Belafonte don't have big lips. *Elvis* got big lips.

DAD: *(To* BILLY*)* Chew on your meat loaf!

(BILLY *hastily does so.*)

DAD: *(To* SHARON*)* You too. Eat your dinner. *(She doesn't move.)* Young lady? *(No response)* I said eat. *(Ominous)* Young. Lady.

SHARON: *(In one breath)* Billy was smoking in the car when we washed it Saturday, and he burned that hole in the seat cover!

MOM: Sharon Ann!

(Beat, as SHARON *picks up fork, jabs food in her mouth)*

*(*BILLY *stabs at* SHARON *under table with fork.)*

DAD: *(To* BILLY*)* You been smokin'? *(No response) (To his wife)* Jesus. What a pair of kids we got.

MOM: *(Angry)* She shouldn't tell tales.

DAD: *(To* BILLY*)* I catch you smokin' and I'll tan your butt. So don't do it again.

BILLY: *(Flip)* O K.

DAD: O K, *who?*

BILLY: *(Military)* O K, *sir.*

DAD: That's better.

(They eat in silence.)

*(*BILLY *and* SHARON *glare at each other)*

SHARON: *(Exasperated; suddenly giggling)* Elvis. Got. Big. Lips.

*(*BILLY *giggles.)*

*(*MOM *smiles, then laughs.)*

*(*DAD *looks at them, then smiles. He raises his hand in mock anger at* BILLY*.)*

*(*BILLY *beams.)*

(They all laugh.)

(Suddenly, at the peak of their laughter:)

(Blackout)

(Soundtrack: The opening bars of Sh-Boom *by the Chords)*

(Music continues into:)

Scene Two

(Afternoon, a month later. Drapes and plate glass doors opened wide. Hot white sunlight.)

(Table is a mess of luncheon remains: a ravaged loaf of Wonder bread, opened jars of peanut butter, jelly, mayonnaise; a pried-open can of Nestle's chocolate syrup, a package of franks, milk carton, dirty glasses, cookies, sandwich rinds.)

(Under music, SHARON runs shrieking into dining room from backyard. She wears a tight, two-piece period bathing suit, which covers her adolescent hips and breasts like bands of shiny steel.)

(A spray of water from offstage. Music out on:)

SHARON: Safety zone!

(BILLY appears in backyard, wearing trunks, dripping wet, holding lawn hose stoppered with finger.)

BILLY: Take your medicine!

SHARON: No. *(Circling table)*

(BILLY releases a jet of water into dining room.)

SHARON: Billy! Not in here!

(BILLY discards hose, enters dining room.)

BILLY: So? What do you care?

SHARON: Just don't, that's all. *(Sits, digs into food)* God. I'm still hungry.

BILLY: What do you care? Mom and Dad'll be in Palm Springs the whole weekend.

SHARON: *(Angrily buttering bread)* Yeah, and I should be too.

BILLY: Then you shouldn't'a snuck out to that sock hop with Dennis.

SHARON: Tough shitsky.

BILLY: After Dad said you couldn't! Two o'clock in the morning!

SHARON: So tough shitsky.

BILLY: *(Mimics)* "Tough shitsky." You *sound* like Dennis.

SHARON: Wish he was here.

BILLY: Dennis been grounded too, ha-ha.

SHARON: Wish it was anybody but *you*.

BILLY: *I* ain't grounded for two whole months, ha-ha.

SHARON: You shoulda been! Dad caught you reading those *National Geographics* in the bathroom!

BILLY: I'm supposed to know anatomy! For art class. *(Sits, digs in)* He was only mad for a minute.

SHARON: *(Disdainfully)* Anatomy. *(Giggles)* All those naked Negroes, what a nurdie.

BILLY: *(Airily)* I coulda gone to Palm Springs if I wanted. I can always go where I want.

SHARON: Goody for you.

BILLY: Only I just hate Palm Springs. All those old golfcarts and fat people.

SHARON: *(Angrily eating)* I coulda gone horseback riding. Swimming. I got a new bathing suit.

BILLY: We'll have fun anyway.

SHARON: No, we won't.

BILLY: *(Impish)* Bread balls.

SHARON: Huh?

BILLY: Like this. *(He takes slice of white bread, extracts the soft center, wads it in fist, rolls it into ball on table.)*

SHARON: *(Giggling)* Put some jelly. *(She extends knife with blob of jelly on it.)*

BILLY: No. Peanut butter. *(He dips ball in jar of peanut butter.)*

SHARON: *And* jelly!

(She smears ball with jelly; he eats it.)

BILLY: *(Laughing through food)* God.

SHARON: Watch. *(She smears bread with mayonnaise.)*

BILLY: Yuckie! A mayonnaise sandwich!

(BILLY watches SHARON eat, her mouth open.)

BILLY: God! You're makin' me sick!

(SHARON eats, bigger.)

BILLY: Sharon! Stop it! O K for you. Look. *(He takes slice of bread, wads it, then squashes and pounds it flat on table.)*

SHARON: What are you doing?

BILLY: Mexican sandwich.

SHARON: A what?

BILLY: Look. *(He lifts flattened bread, dips it in can of chocolate syrup.)*

SHARON: *(Watching him)* What a weirdio!

(BILLY pops dripping concoction in mouth.)

BILLY: Yum. Meeee.

SHARON: *(Disgusted)* Dum. Meeee.

BILLY: *(Leaning towards her)* They'd hate it if they saw us!

SHARON: *(Giggling)* Yeah! *(Reaches for milk carton; pours)* Watch. *(She drinks entire glass, the liquid dribbling down chin onto breasts. Finishes with a flourish)* Milkstache!

BILLY: *(Laughing)* What?

SHARON: Dennis *loves* licking off my milkstache. *(She indicates upper lip.)* That's what he calls it. From the milk.

BILLY: *(Contemptuously)* Clev-errrr.

SHARON: Shut up.

BILLY: Watch this. *(He spills a little milk onto table, mixes in some jelly.)*

SHARON: Billy!

BILLY: *(Finger painting)* It's a painting! *(Smears)* This is Dennis' hair. *(Adds cookies)* And his ears. And— *(Takes a weinie)* His nose. *(Takes another)* And down here—

SHARON: Don't be *dirty!* God.

BILLY: So lemme draw *you!*

SHARON: No.

BILLY: I mean a *real* picture. I'm gettin' good, you'll see.

(SHARON casually brushes milk off breasts and adjusts top of suit as:)

SHARON: I dunno. Maybe.

BILLY: Please. Pretty please? With mayonnaise on it?

SHARON: *(Fluffing hair)* Oh. I dunno. *(Throws cookie at him)* O K.

BILLY: *(Rising)* I'll get my stuff! *(He exits.)*

(SHARON licks lips, puts hands to hips, raises shoulders cheese-cake style, and belches.)

(Giggling, she leans forward and runs finger through guck on table.)

(Reenter BILLY with pad and crayons. He sits, crayon poised.)

BILLY: O K. Pose for me. Something sexy. Something low-rider.

(SHARON puts finger to cheek, wide-eyed innocence.)

BILLY: What's that?

SHARON: Annette.

BILLY: Who?

SHARON: Annette Funicello. *(No response; drops pose. No response; finger to cheek)* So draw me.

BILLY: That ain't sexy.

SHARON: So this. *(She spins around, straddling chair; waves.)* Back of a motorcycle.

BILLY: That's a little better. Try something else.

SHARON: O K. *(She rises, sits on edge of table, hugging shoulders. Pouts cutely)* Oooh.

BILLY: What's that? That "oooh"?

SHARON: Models. They all do that. *(Pouts)* Draw it.

BILLY: *(Drawing)* They don't neither. "Oooh."

SHARON: They do too.

BILLY: *(Contemptuously)* Annette Mouseketeer.

SHARON: *(Dropping pose)* Oh, you don't know anything. Here. *(She leans back onto table, propping herself with palms, among the half-eaten sandwiches, legs crossed, classic bathing beauty pose.)*

BILLY: You keep changing!

SHARON: *(Thrusting up breasts)* Ooooh.

(BILLY stares.)

BILLY: Wow. *(Ripping out sheet, starting another)* That's bitchin'. *(Draws)*

SHARON: *Seventeen.*

BILLY: *(Drawing rapidly)* Huh?

SHARON: Someday. I'm gonna be on the cover of *Seventeen.*

BILLY: *(Snickering as he draws)* With those big old knockers?

SHARON: *(Tensing)* Shut up.

BILLY: That's why you're so popular. That's why Dennis likes you.

SHARON: That's mean! *(Abruptly dropping pose, she sits up, crossing arms over her breasts.)*

BILLY: Sharon, stop changing! That was sexy!

SHARON: You're just. I dunno. Stupoid.

BILLY: But it was real low-rider!

SHARON: Yeah, well you're a brain!

BILLY: Who is?

SHARON: *(Taunting)* Everybody at North says. Billy. Is a brain.

BILLY: Am not.

SHARON: Are too.

BILLY: Not!

SHARON: Are.

BILLY: Dad says you're just a greasy, cheap, low-rider Pachuco slut!

(SHARON springs angrily from table.)

SHARON: Dennis says you're queer!

(BILLY freezes. SHARON sits, tears into food.)

BILLY: What?

SHARON: My creepo brother!

BILLY: What. Did Dennis say?

SHARON: Nobody likes you!

(BILLY discards pad and crayon onto floor, rises.)

BILLY: God. They catch you reading a book and. *(Crosses to plate glass; looks out)* God.

SHARON: *(Blithely)* You're just a farmer, that's all.

BILLY: No. You.

SHARON: *(Singsong)* Four-eyed farmer and a queerio.

BILLY: Pachuco sluttio.

SHARON: *(Laughing through food)* Brain farmer.

BILLY: *(Also laughing)* Grease rider chiquita.

SHARON: *(Same)* Teacher pet face.

BILLY: *(Same)* Mexi-nose.

SHARON: *Let's draw Dad!*

BILLY: Bitchin'! *(She springs for drawing stuff on floor and scoots under table.)*

(BILLY joins her.)

SHARON: *(Giggling; drawing)* In his undershirt.

BILLY: *(Taking pad and crayon)* No, Sharon. Like this. See?

SHARON: *(Watching him draw)* Yeah. In the vibrating chair.

BILLY: Yeah. Or this.

SHARON: What's—?

BILLY: Like when he walks around the house naked.

(She grabs pad away.)

SHARON: Not that. Not dirty.

BILLY: O K. O K. *(Retrieves pad; draws)* In his work boots. Scratching himself. Skin problems.

SHARON: Give him green spots.

BILLY: And this is you.

SHARON: Huh?

BILLY: As a stewardess. Dad's in a plane in a vibrating seat and you're serving him coffee and this— *(Crayon slides off pad onto her knee)* —is the Rockies. You're flyin' over the Rockies.

SHARON: *(Giggling)* Where we going?

BILLY: To Memphis. To marry Elvis. And so you keep flying— *(Crayon up her thigh)*

SHARON: That tickles, dummie!

BILLY: And flying and now you're over— *(Crayon stright up her hip, midriff, to breasts)* The Grand Tetons!

SHARON: Stop it!

(Crayon jumps to her shoulder.)

BILLY: O K! The pretty hills of Nebraska and— *(Along her shoulder to clavicle and up her neck)* The beautiful Colorado gorge and— *(To her mouth)* The Black Hole of Kansas!

(SHARON grabs crayon and colors BILLY's nose.)

SHARON: And this is Albuquerque!

BILLY: O K, where else?

(Crayon down his chin, neck)

SHARON: And this is Chicken Neck, Arkansas—

BILLY: *(Giggling)* Shut up.

(Crayon down shoulders and chest)

SHARON: And Chicken Wing, Tennessee, and Chicken Ribs, North Dakota—

BILLY: Keep going.

(Crayon to his belly)

SHARON: Little Pot, Montana, and—

(BILLY pushes crayon downward.)

BILLY: And that's where Elvis lives!

(Shocked, SHARON drops crayon.)

SHARON: Billy! You shouldn't do that *in public!*

(She turns away as he quickly draws up his legs.)

SHARON: God. You're worse than Dennis.

BILLY: *(Delighted)* I am?

SHARON: Least he tries to *hide* his.

BILLY: Really?

SHARON: God. *(She starts doodling on pad.)*

BILLY: It felt good, that's all. *(Beat)* I'm sorry.

SHARON: Shut up and report to the vice principal.

BILLY: What you drawing?

SHARON: Nothing. I'm dreaming

BILLY: What about?

SHARON: Oh. A beautiful place.

BILLY: That's nice. Boy. *(He props his chin on her shoulder.)* I'd rather be with you. Than anybody.

(Beat; SHARON doodles on, her head against BILLY's.)

SHARON: Billy?

BILLY: Hmmm?

SHARON: Dad didn't really. Call me a slut. Did he?

BILLY: Dad. He got rocks in his head.

SHARON: He said that? Right out loud?

BILLY: He was just mad you stayed out so late. *(Beat)* You're the best sister in California.

(SHARON closes her eyes, hums a dance tune, languidly doodles.)

SHARON: I can see a sock hop palace.

BILLY: Yeah? And what else?

SHARON: All these kids. Laughing. And me in the middle. Dancing.

(She hums softly, eyes closed, his head on her shoulder.)

BILLY: With me, Sharon? Would you dance with me?

(She ceases to hum. Opens her eyes. Tears are welling.)

SHARON: I'm not. A slut.

(SHARON reaches out blindly for her brother, who hugs her to him.)

(Clutching at each other, they sink full-length onto the floor, a tangle of awkward limbs.)

(Lights slowly dim to black as:)

(Sound track: the opening bars of Sorry (I Ran All the Way Home) *by the Impalas)*

(Music fades. Lights up on:)

Scene Three

(Dinnertime, three months later. Drapes partially drawn)

(MOM is sitting at table, head in hands, SHARON sitting across from her. Sheepishly:)

SHARON: Oh, mother. *(Silence)* Say something. *(Silence. Groping:)* I can't. This is. *(Silence)* Yell at me. Say you hate me or. *(Silence)* You hate me.

MOM: You. Ignatz! *(She rises, turns, sits down again, face in hands.)* I could use. A filthy word.

SHARON: I guess you should say it.

MOM: Your father. Will go through the roof.

SHARON: Yell at me. I would. If I was you.

MOM: *(Looking at daughter)* How would you know?

SHARON: What?

MOM: What I feel. How would— *(Pause)* —you know?

SHARON: I can't say I'm sorry fifty times.

MOM: I don't believe it.

SHARON: Maybe she's wrong.

MOM: *(Hastily)* The school nurse? What did she say?

SHARON: I told you.

MOM: Oh. *(Beat)* We could. Wait. For the tests.

SHARON: We don't have to tell Daddy now.

MOM: No.

SHARON: Do we?

(MOM rises, exits into kitchen.)

(SHARON fidgets.)

MOM: *(From kitchen)* Which one was it? Sharon? *(She reenters with coffee cup.)* You see so many boys. Was it Dennis?

SHARON: I guess so.

MOM: You guess?

SHARON: Yes. Dennis.

MOM: How. Many. Boys. Have you. *(She plops into chair.)* Through the roof.

(MOM and SHARON sit staring in silence.)

(Enter BILLY, left. Throws books on table)

BILLY: *(Spluttering like a souped-up auto)* Tuck 'n roll. *(Gear shift sound)* Taco balls. *(Peeling tires sound)* The Marquis. *(He exits into kitchen.)*

(MOM and SHARON sit in silence.)

BILLY: *(From kitchen)* Mom? Next year I get a car, right?

MOM: *(Dully)* Right.

BILLY: *(Sticking his head out of kitchen)* Right?

MOM: *(Angrily)* Right!

BILLY: *(Same)* O K. O K. You don't haveta bite my face off. *(Disappears into kitchen. From there:)* Dad looked at this '54 Chevy I don't want that. A '56 maybe. That's cherry. I could get into a car club with that. *(Re-enters with sandwich, sits)* A plaque. See it through the rear window. The Marquis. Or the Monarchs.

SHARON: The Creeps.

MOM: Sharon!

(SHARON looks at MOM, then at BILLY.)

SHARON: *(Mimics her brother)* "The Monarchs." Fat chance.

BILLY: Shut up.

(SHARON begins to giggle, a tad hysterically.)

SHARON: "The Marquis, the Monarchs." Who would cruise with *you*? You and some skag. Two fudds in some old '54 Chevy. "The Fudds." You could join "The Fudds." Two four-eyed-creepo-scaggy-*brains*! *(She bangs fist on table; covers face with hands.)*

(BILLY and MOM stare at SHARON.)

MOM: Sharon *Ann*!

BILLY: God. What did *I* do?

MOM: *(To BILLY)* Go out and play.

BILLY: Go out and play what?

MOM: *(Ominously)* Go. Read. A book.

(SHARON looks at ceiling; a curt laugh.)

SHARON: Yeah. A book.

(BILLY gazes from one to the other, puts half-eaten sandwich in mouth, gathers up books.)

BILLY: *(Looking at them; through sandwich)* God. *(He exits, left.)*

(Silence)

MOM: We could say, maybe. But we're not sure yet.

SHARON: *(Shaking her head)* Oh, mother.

MOM: And Dennis' parents. We'll have to talk to them.

SHARON: *(Same)* Stop.

MOM: We'll have to send you back east. Your grandmother.

SHARON: I don't care.

MOM: That. Is. Obvious. *(Rises, turns to enter kitchen, pauses)* I should fix something. For dinner. I should fix. Liver.

SHARON: *(Toneless)* And onions.

MOM: Lots of onions.

SHARON: *(Bitterly sarcastic)* Billy hates onions.

MOM: He can eat a frozen. How many, Sharon?

SHARON: What?

MOM: How many boys? *(No response)* You tell your father. Only Dennis.

SHARON: That's. Cootie.

MOM: That's what?

SHARON: Not fair.

MOM: Does Dennis know about. Any other boys?

SHARON: *(Quickly)* No.

MOM: Then *only Dennis.* You better tell him that.

(MOM exits into kitchen.)

(SHARON sits in silence, smoothing her petticoats.)

(Sound of a door slamming)

(SHARON hastily rises, exits into kitchen.)

(Enter DAD, in soiled work clothes, carrying tin lunch pail. He is tired.)

DAD: *(Calling)* Sweetheart?

MOM: *(From kitchen)* Take a bath.

DAD: *(Sitting; lunch pail on table)* Gimme a whiskey and water first.

MOM: O K.

DAD: *(Afterthought)* Sweetie.

MOM: O K.

(DAD lights cigarette, exhales slowly, begins untying caked workman's boots—all punctuated with groans of fatigue.)

(MOM enters with drink.)

DAD: *(Taking drink)* Oh, woman. You don't know. *(Drinks deeply, sounds of pleasure)*

MOM: Honey, um.

DAD: *(Looking at her)* You been crying?

MOM: Chopping onions. We're having liver and onions.

DAD: Hey now. Is that right? I'll be goddamned.

MOM: You can't even see the liver. All those onions.

DAD: *(Rubbing hands together)* Goddamn. Ol' Dad gets his favorite. *(Beat)* Why?

MOM: What?

DAD: Well, *somethin's* gotta be wrong. I get my favorite.

(MOM laughs nervously.)

(Beat)

MOM: There is.

DAD: So?

(Beat)

MOM: After dinner.

DAD: I said: So?

MOM: We'll talk later.

DAD: Sharon or Billy?

MOM: Sharon. After dinner, honey. We'll talk.

DAD: Where is she?

MOM: In the kitchen.

(DAD *rises.*)

MOM: Leave her alone.

(DAD *stares at* MOM; *sits.*)

DAD: Bring her in here. *(Beat)* Now.

(MOM *hesitates, then exits into kitchen.*)

(DAD *places lunch pail on floor and clasps his hands before him, waiting.*)

(MOM *reenters,* SHARON *slowly following.*)

DAD: *(To* SHARON*)* Well, young lady. *(Silence)* I said. Well, young lady.

SHARON: I heard you.

(Pause)

DAD: You heard me. Good. *(To his wife)* She heard me. *(To* SHARON*)* So answer me.

MOM: Honey.

DAD: Let her tell it.

MOM: It happens, honey, it's—

DAD: *(Banging table)* Shut up! Let. Her. Tell it.

MOM: She's ignatz.

(DAD *stares at* MOM.*)

DAD: *(Grotesquely mimics his wife)* "She's ignatz! She's ignatz!"

MOM: Honey, don't get—

DAD: *(Gesturing wildly)* "Ignatz! Ignatz!"

SHARON: *(Quickly)* I'm gonna—!

(DAD ceases, stares at his daughter.)

SHARON: Gonna have a baby.

(Pause)

DAD: You. What?

SHARON: I told you.

DAD: Say it again. I didn't hear this.

MOM: *(Dropping into a chair)* The high school nurse, honey. Only. There's no tests. I mean—

DAD: I didn't *hear* this!

SHARON: Oh, Daddy.

DAD: *(To SHARON)* You let some boy. Put his. Up *you*? *(Beat; he leans across table towards her.)* Is that what you said? *(Beat)* You said. Some boy. Put his. His filthy. Up *you*? *(Beat)* You said that, right? *(No response; he draws back.)* Jesus Christ.

(They all stare down at table.)

MOM: We'll send her to your mother's. In Chicago. We'll put it up for adoption.

DAD: Like a dog. *(Beat)* I work like a dog. *(Looks up at SHARON)* You know what that means? *(No response)* No, you don't. It means. *(Springing to his feet; loudly)* That I got Mexicans all day! *(Sits again; gestures helplessly)* Means we hadda dig a ditch today. Uphill. Twenny-four inch pipeline San Onofre. *Up! Hill! (Waves his hand, indicating house)* To give you all this.

MOM: *(Jumping up)* Liver's burning.

(MOM hastily exits into kitchen.)

DAD: *(Continuing to SHARON)* And you walk up to me. And you squat here. And crap. All over. *(Beat)* I come home from work and there's this crap on my table.

MOM: *(From kitchen)* Sharon? Set the table.

(SHARON goes in and out of kitchen, setting table, DAD watching her. As she reenters:)

DAD: Some hood I'll bet. One of those hoods you go out with.

(SHARON exits; reenters.)

DAD: Duck-butt. Right? Pimples.

(SHARON exits; reenters.)

DAD: You like that. Pimples. *(Beat) Answer me!*

(SHARON stands still, not looking at DAD.)

(MOM hastily reenters, spatula in hand.)

MOM: Dennis. It was that Dennis.

DAD: That who?

MOM: Blond kid. Drives that candy apple.

(Exit MOM into kitchen.)

DAD: *(To SHARON; contemptuously)* Den. Nis.

(SHARON exits into kitchen.)

(DAD drains his whiskey and water.)

(MOM reenters, coffee pot in hand.)

MOM: You want coffee?

DAD: This Dennis. Has gotta marry her.

MOM: *(Filling his cup)* They're too young, honey. Your mother's. Back east.

(SHARON reenters, setting table. DAD watches her.)

DAD: Your boyfriend. Is gonna have to drop outa school. Get himself a job. And pay for this.

MOM: Honey, that's—

DAD: *And pay for this! (Beat)* Where's the cream?

MOM: I'll get it.

DAD: No! Sharon's gonna get it. *(To* SHARON*)* Get it.

*(*SHARON, *on verge of tears, exits into kitchen.)*

MOM: How can she marry him? What can he do, he's a kid like her?

DAD: Quiet.

MOM: *We'll* end up supporting them.

DAD: I said. Quiet.

(Reenter SHARON. *Extends milk carton to* DAD*)*

DAD: *(To* SHARON*)* Pour it in.

*(*SHARON *shakily pours; spills it.)*

DAD: Uh-oh. You spilt it. *(Beat)* Uh-oh.

*(*SHARON *gestures helplessly with carton, at a loss.)*

DAD: *(Deadly)* So clean it up.

*(*SHARON *closes her eyes, fighting tears.)*

MOM: I'll get a sponge.

DAD: No! Her. *(To* SHARON*)* Get a sponge and clean it up.

*(*SHARON *sets down carton; exits into kitchen.)*

MOM: Honey.

*(*DAD *is staring after* SHARON.*)*

MOM: It happens.

*(*DAD *doesn't respond.)*

(Reenter SHARON *with sponge; sops up mess, starts to exit.)*

DAD: Hey.

*(*SHARON *pauses, her back to* DAD.*)*

DAD: I don't want this coffee it's ruint. *(Beat)* Take it away. Get me another cup.

*(*SHARON *turns back to table.)*

DAD: You gotta get use to this. A brat on one tittie and a sponge in your hand.

(SHARON *takes cup.*)

DAD: Get use to it.

(*Exit* SHARON *with cup.*)

MOM: I'll get— (*Despairingly puts coffee pot on table*) Dinner.

(MOM *exits as* SHARON *reenters with clean cup.*)

(DAD *watches as* SHARON *replaces cup and tries shakily to pour coffee into it.*)

DAD: You spilt it again!

(SHARON *puts down pot; closes eyes.*)

DAD: I don't believe this. You can't even pour coffee. And you was gonna go. You was gonna go to stewardess school? You woulda flunked out.

(SHARON *sets down pot.*)

(*Reenter* MOM *with plate of food.*)

DAD: (*To* SHARON, *pointing at cup*) Girls who whoor around—

MOM: (*Disapproving*) Honey!

DAD: (*To* MOM) You got a nicer word for it? (*To* SHARON; *resuming:*) —Should learn to pour coffee!

(SHARON *reaches for his cup.*)

DAD: (*To* SHARON) Never mind!

(MOM *places plate before* DAD.)

DAD: A girl cheap enough to get pregnant is too cheap. To pour my coffee.

MOM: Get Billy, Sharon.

SHARON: Daddy? (*Beat. She can't look at him.*) Stop.

DAD: (*Feigned innocence*) Stop what?

SHARON: Stop it. I'm. I'm sorry. I wish I was dead.

DAD: You're sorry. *(To* MOM*)* She wishes she was dead. *(To* SHARON*)* I don't wish that. I just wish you wasn't. *(Beat)* So cheap.

SHARON: Please, Daddy.

DAD: You make us cheap? O K. You crap on us? We can live with that. You don't care about us? Fine. But you. *(Points his knife at her)* Don't care about yourself. That's what hurts. *(Looks at plate)* That's what hurts your Daddy.

MOM: Dinner's getting cold. Sharon, go get Billy. *(She exits into kitchen.)*

SHARON: *(Fighting tears)* I'll never do it again.

DAD: *(Exploding) I for chrissakes hope not!*

(Reenter MOM *with two plates; to her:)*

DAD: Never do it again. That's funny. This daughter we got? She's *cheap.* But she's funny. *(Beat; to* SHARON*)* How many times?

(Beat; MOM *pauses to stare at* DAD*.)*

DAD: How many times you do it with him? This Den. Nis pimple. Huh?

MOM: *(Level voice; setting down plates)* Sharon. Call your brother.

DAD: *(Rising from chair)* I wanna know! *(He collars* SHARON*; into her face.)* How. Many. Times.

SHARON: *(Struggling against him)* Daddy.

MOM: *(Clenching fists)* Honey? It's time for dinner!

DAD: *(Bearing down on* SHARON*)* Once? Twice?

SHARON: Mother!

MOM: I said it's time for dinner!

DAD: (*Same*) Six times? (*He has* SHARON *painfully by nape of neck.*) I gotta right to know. Fifty? Just nod your head.

MOM: Leave her alone!

DAD: (*Same*) She was goin' to some *sock hop*? Some movie? (*Mimics*) "Bye, Daddy." You say, "Bye, I'm goin' to a football game."

MOM: (*Grabbing his arm*) You're hurting her!

DAD: (*Shrugging off* MOM ; *spinning* SHARON *against table*) So it's tough shit, Daddy, tough (*He slaps* SHARON *once.*) —shit— (*Twice*) —Daddy!

(MOM *forces herself between them; pushes* DAD *away.*)

MOM: This is Sharon! (*Into his face*) You're doing this. To *Sharon!*

(MOM *embraces* SHARON, *who is stunned, blinded, tears welling.*)

(DAD *stares at them, then abruptly sits, cuts up liver, breathing hard. To them, through his food:*)

DAD: Sit down. Sit. Down. And eat.

(*Enter* BILLY *noisily, making motor sounds.*)

BILLY: Dinner ready yet?

MOM: (*Easing* SHARON *into chair*) It's ready. Come to the table.

(*Looking hard at* DAD, MOM *exits into kitchen.*)

BILLY: (*Approaching table*) Hi, Dad.

(DAD *does not respond; he is shoveling food into his mouth and staring at* SHARON.)

(BILLY *sits at table. Sees food*)

BILLY: Yuckie. *Liver*?

(SHARON *is looking blindly before her.*)

DAD: *(To* SHARON*)* Eat.

*(*SHARON *does not respond.)*

DAD: Girls who act cheap gotta eat everything on her plate.

BILLY: *Liver?* God.

(Enter MOM *with T V dinner.)*

MOM: *(To* BILLY*)* Don't get antsy. You get a frozen.

*(*MOM *seats herself. They all eat in silence, except for* SHARON, *who stares at plate.* DAD *hasn't taken his eyes from her. Through his food:)*

DAD: Girls who get in trouble. Should eat. What we put in front of her.

*(*SHARON *blindly picks up fork.)*

DAD: I said. Girls who shame her Daddy should eat her dinner.

*(*SHARON *lifts forkful of onions to her mouth; pauses.)*

DAD: Should put it in her mouth.

*(*SHARON *does so.)*

DAD: And eat.

*(*SHARON *chews slowly. Swallows)*

DAD: All of it. *(Beat)* Eat it all. *(Beat)* I wanna see a clean plate. Like the plate was washed. Clean. *(Beat)* You. Are gonna. *(Beat)* Lick it. *(Beat)* Clean.

*(*SHARON *drops fork, covers her mouth; chokes into napkin.)*

DAD: Hey! I worked hard for that food.

MOM: *(To her husband)* Stop it. Now.

DAD: *(To his wife; still looking at* SHARON*)* What?

MOM: I said. Stop it.

DAD: (*Looking at his wife; wide-eyed innocence*) But I worked for that. She craps on me and now she throws up my food?

MOM: Just stop it. *Please.*

DAD: Come on, Sharon. Girls like you. You crap and throw up on your Daddies at the same time? Not. Nice. Now try again.

(SHARON *puts down her napkin; slowly, she follows his instructions:*)

DAD: Take your fork. And your knife. Cut the meat. Cut it up. That's right. Now put it in your mouth. Here.

(DAD *reaches across table for* SHARON'*s hand, forces her to gather onions on her fork.*)

DAD: Put some onions with it. Cram some onions in there.

(DAD *guides fork into* SHARON'*s mouth; she does not chew.*)

BILLY: (*Staring*) God.

DAD: (*Withdrawing hand; to* SHARON) Now. Swallow it. (*Beat*) Swallow it all.

(SHARON *attempts to do so, fighting back the sobs.*)

(*She chokes.*)

DAD: (*Warningly*) Don't you do it again! I worked hard for that.

(SHARON *can't help it; upchucks into napkin.*)

DAD: You did it again! You puked on me again! Here.

(DAD *reaches across table again and grabs* SHARON'S *hand.*)

DAD: Now you gotta start all over!

(*Using free hand,* SHARON *stabs the back of* DAD'*s hand with her knife.*)

(DAD *yells, recoiling.*)

DAD: Jesus!

SHARON: *(Screaming)* I hate you!

DAD: *(Holding out hand to his wife)* Look what she did!

(MOM covers her face with hands.)

SHARON: *(Same)* You're having me for dinner! *(She buries her face in her napkin, sobbing.)*

(A long pause)

(DAD rises from chair, rubbing his hand. He looks fearfully at SHARON.)

(Exit DAD, left.)

(Front door slams, off.)

(Silence)

BILLY: God.

MOM: *(Rising from chair; to BILLY)* Finish your.

(Shaking her head, MOM exits into kitchen.)

(BILLY and SHARON sit in silence.)

BILLY: Sharon? *(Beat)* What did you do? *(Beat)* Huh?

(SHARON manages to stand.)

SHARON: *(Hand over stomach)* My room. Lay down. *(She slowly crosses left.)*

BILLY: God. You musta done something. Bad.

(SHARON pauses at doorway. Turns, hisses at BILLY)

SHARON: *It's yours!*

(Exit SHARON, quickly, left.)

(BILLY stares after her.)

(Blackout)

(Sound track: the opening bars of Little Star *by the Elegants)*

(Music fades. Lights up on:)

Scene Four

(*A Saturday afternoon, six months later. Drapes are open, and sunlight floods the room.*)

(MOM *is setting table for lunch. She is in and out of kitchen. Goes to plate glass door, opens it.*)

MOM: (*Calling*) Honeee? Billeee? Lunch! (*She exits into kitchen.*)

(*Beat*)

(DAD *and* BILLY *enter, in greasy clothes, through plate glass door.*)

BILLY: (*Looking at greasy hands*) Icky.

DAD: You gotta expect to get dirty workin' on cars. (*Pours himself a drink from bottle on table*) Go wash up.

BILLY: How come we hadda grease it? You just bought it.

DAD: You should care about your machine. Treat it good and it'll run for your whole life.

BILLY: I gotta drive a '54 Chevy 'til I'm *forty*?

DAD: (*Drinking*) It was a good buy. For the money. Kid like you it's O K.

BILLY: (*Muttering*) A '56 woulda been O K. (*He exits into kitchen.*)

DAD: (*Calling after him*) You wanted some M G like that Becker kid? Who's a spoiled rotten snotface?

(*Enter* MOM *with sandwiches; to her:*)

DAD: It's not good enough.

MOM: It's a car.

DAD: For the money? It's a great car.

MOM: It's a car. He can drive to Hollywood. And the beach.

DAD: Hollywood? Downey ain't good enough?

MOM: *(Deprecating)* Honey.

DAD: Sunset Strip for chrissakes and then what?

MOM: Go wash your hands.

DAD: It's a good car.

MOM: I know that. Billy's different, that's all.

DAD: He's what?

MOM: That's all. He's more serious.

DAD: Than what?

MOM: Than Sharon. And other kids. He's brainier.

DAD: *(Laughing bitterly)* Hell, Sharon got brains. Only they're between her boobies. Which is why—

MOM: So he's different, that's all.

DAD: She's back east havin' a kid.

MOM: Be quiet. Billy.

DAD: He knows. Everybody knows. *(Points at sandwiches)* That better not be Spam.

MOM: It's ham. Ham and liverwurst. He could be a teacher. He gets very good grades.

DAD: Except in math. He's a boneskull in math. Now Sharon? *(Raises his glass)* Coulda gone to airline school. You know what that means? She coulda flown around like a queen. *(Drains glass; grabs a sandwich)* For free. With benefits.

MOM: Wash your hands.

DAD: *(Munching)* It's the wave of the future. People flyin' to New Jersey like we drive to Covina. And this! She passes up.

MOM: She can still apply. Later.

DAD: She better straighten up back there.

MOM: She can still graduate with her class it's all fixed.

DAD: Airlines ain't gonna hire some girl that screws around.

MOM: I said be quiet.

DAD: You gotta be spotless.

MOM: They won't know.

DAD: That brochure they sent us? They want perfect reputations and a particular kinna build even. She was too topheavy as it was. They give physicals, you know.

MOM: *Wash your hands!*

(Beat)

DAD: O K. O K.

(DAD puts down sandwich. Exits into kitchen as BILLY *passes out of it)*

BILLY: *(Looking at hands)* Greasy gook. I scrubbed so hard I'm bleeding.

MOM: I'm going shopping. You want anything special?

BILLY: *(Sitting at table)* Yeah. A '56 Chevy.

MOM: Don't complain, ignatz. It's a car, isn't it?

BILLY: A klunky dork on wheels. *(Picks up sandwich)* Pukey! *Liver?*

MOM: Liver*wurst*. And ham. I made two ham.

BILLY: How can you tell? What if I went and bit *into* it?

(MOM, shaking her head, goes to kitchen door.)

MOM: Honey? I'm going shopping. See you later.

DAD: *(From kitchen)* O K, sweetie.

BILLY: *(Mimics)* "O K, sweetie."

MOM: *(Batting him affectionately)* Pipe down.

(Exit MOM, left.)

(Silence, as BILLY *carefully bites into a sandwich.)*

(Enter DAD.*)*

DAD: *(Sitting, with a sigh)* Oh my my my my my.

BILLY: *(Indicating sandwich plate)* Liverwurst. I get ham.

DAD: Better not be Spam, that's all. Ever since the Army, I can't eat Spam.

BILLY: Me neither.

DAD: Don't be cute at me. *(Eating)* You should pray you never have to fight. *(Beat)* Army'd whip you into shape. *(Beat)* War. It's a terrible thing.

BILLY: Long's I don't haveta grease cars.

DAD: Cutemouth. *(Puts down sandwich)* Now. After lunch? We gonna go over that engine. I want you to know plugs. Points. Carburetor. Pistons. And how they connect up. Here. *(Takes a pad and clip pencil out of his breast pocket)*

BILLY: Dad? I'm eating here.

DAD: *(Drawing in pad)* O K. Here's the block.

BILLY: The what?

DAD: The block. The basic gut of your car. It cracks and you can throw the whole thing away.

BILLY: Dad?

DAD: Now inside the block. Depending of course on if it's a V-8 or a -6—

BILLY: Did you date girls in Chicago?

(Beat)

DAD: What?

BILLY: When you was a kid.

*(*DAD *stares at* BILLY.*)*

DAD: And the points. Inside the block. Gotta be ignited.

BILLY: Can I get it painted at least? That turdy green and offwhite it's like—

DAD: *(Slamming down pencil) Who cares! What it looks like? (Beat)* A thing. On the outside? Is nothin'! It's the inside of a thing that counts. You gotta know. How a thing works. Put your hands in there and. *(Gropes)* Make sure it's workin' right. Some smartass ridin' around don't know the inside of his car? Is prob'ly a careless stupid who stands there! On the side of the freeway. With his fire-engine red busted-down Buick and cryin'! Like a. *(Gropes. Into his son's face)* Like a *woman!*

(Beat)

(BILLY *is staring down at plate.)*

(DAD *eats.)*

DAD: Finish your sandwich.

(BILLY *nibbles, looking down.)*

DAD: You got dating on your mind?

BILLY: *(Resentfully)* Why do you think I want the car?

DAD: So. All this I just told you. I should yack at the lamps. *(Beat)* A car ain't for *cruisin'. (Beat)* A car? Is for a use.

BILLY: Girls are a use.

DAD: You ain't even got a learner's permit yet. You can't pick up girls anyhow, so stop thinkin' about it.

(BILLY *and* DAD *eat.)*

(Pause)

DAD: When I was in the Army?

BILLY: Yeah?

DAD: You can catch things.

BILLY: What things?

DAD: Things. You gotta be careful. Little crawly things.

BILLY: *(Eagerly)* Yeah? In the Army?

DAD: Toilet seats. Towels. Sometimes on people's bodies. Girls too.

BILLY: Yeah? Where on girls?

DAD: They're everywhere. You can get 'em off anything. You only got this one body, so keep it clean.

BILLY: Wow. You got cooties off a *girl*?

DAD: Just be careful, that's all! They got medicine it's not a federal case. Forget I said it. *(Beat)* Just be careful.

BILLY: Wow.

(BILLY *and* DAD *eat in silence.*)

BILLY: So what else?

DAD: What else what?

(DAD *puts down his sandwich and starts to draw.* BILLY *watches him.*)

DAD: This. Is your carburetor.

BILLY: Dad? When was the first time you did it? Was it in a car?

(DAD *angrily slams down pencil.*)

DAD: What are you, a moron?

BILLY: Was it with Mom?

DAD: What?

BILLY: What's the girl feel?

DAD: What do you care?

BILLY: But Dad. We never. Talked about this.

DAD: O K! *(Shrugs)* So now you know.

BILLY: O K.

(DAD *resumes drawing,* BILLY *watching him.*)

(DAD *shows him drawing.*)

DAD: So this. Like I said. It's a carburetor. Which mixes your gas and some air. It sits underneath the air cleaner, O K? *(Draws)* Here's the air cleaner.

BILLY: *(Impish; pointing)* What's that?

DAD: I'll get to that. So the choke plate on the carb lets in the air—

BILLY: Can I see your pencil?

DAD: What?

(BILLY *takes pencil; draws.*)

DAD: What are you doing?

BILLY: Air. I'm drawing in the air. Little circles. See?

DAD: *(Yanking away pencil)* Gimme the pencil. *(Referring to drawing)* Now in the old days we had manual chokes but now it's automatic. You gotta have like a sixteen-to-one air-to-gas ratio for idling, and then you want like twelve to thirteen parts air to go full throttle.

BILLY: What's that there?

DAD: That's a cam, I'll get to that. Now all this gotta be adjusted or you can't start your car in the morning. So these solenoids—

BILLY: *(Giggling)* Solenoids?

DAD: Yeah?

BILLY: Sounds weird. Like. *(Beat)* Hey, you stupid solenoid.

DAD: Would you pay attention here?

(BILLY *grabs pencil from* DAD.)

BILLY: *(Drawing)* You should shade in this part. Gives you depth. See?

DAD: *(Angrily; grabbing pencil back)* What are you, Walt Disney? *(Beat)* I got this car so you could learn about it before you start drivin'. I don't want my kid out there hot roddin' around like a moron with *no respect* for what it is.

BILLY: You can't cherry around in no '54 Chevy.

DAD: *(Repressing his anger)* Now, this air cleaner sits up here and it got a filter. You gotta have clean air in your system or you gonna misfire it could be dangerous on the freeway. So you change that filter when it gets dirty. Remember that, in the fuel system of your car, cleanliness is next to godliness.

BILLY: Sure.

DAD: And a two-barrel carb is a damn expensive thing so you gotta keep all your adjustments right. You got the idle circuit, the acceleration circuit—

BILLY: Is Sharon gonna drive the car?

(Beat)

DAD: What?

BILLY: When she gets back. You gonna tell her all this?

DAD: She's a *girl*! She can drive it, sure. But basically it's gonna be your responsibility. You keep it runnin' good and it won't break down on her. A girl out there in a broke-down car? Is like helpless. You want your sister out there all helpless?

(Beat)

BILLY: No.

DAD: So pay attention. *(Points at drawing)* So what's this?

BILLY: A solenoid?

DAD: *(Shaking head)* This! is a solenoid. Here. Is the choke plate.

BILLY: The way you draw I can't tell. There's no contrast or nothin'. *(Takes pencil)* See, if you just put some shadow here then—

DAD: *You want the back of my hand?*

(BILLY drops pencil.)

(DAD pours himself a shot, drinks it.)

(Silence)

DAD: *(Not looking at* BILLY*)* When I was a kid I woulda died to have a car. I usta hang around garages just to look inside 'em.

(Silence)

BILLY: Dad?

DAD: Finish your sandwich.

BILLY: Remember that time you gave me a shot of whiskey and I threw up?

DAD: *(Smiles)* Yeah. *(Sententious)* Drinkin's like drivin'. Kids shouldn't do it. So you learned somethin' that time. *(Points at drawing)* I wish you'd learn somethin' here.

(Beat)

BILLY: Remember when you usta walk around naked in front of us? And told Sharon to look at you?

(DAD stares at BILLY.*)*

DAD: You're a moron.

BILLY: But you did.

DAD: So? It's O K when kids are little. Kids can take a gander it's a natural thing to know.

BILLY: But Mom didn't.

DAD: For chrissakes! You want your mother walkin' around here like a naked floozy?

BILLY: No.

DAD: Why'd you bring that up?

BILLY: What up?

DAD: That about me. Why?

BILLY: I dunno.

DAD: What's goin' on in your head? (*Rises from chair*) I'm startin' to think you're kinna funny like.

(DAD *crosses to plate glass. Looks out at yard. Lights a cigarette*)

(BILLY *looks down at plate.*)

DAD: (*Over his shoulder*) And I don't mean ha-ha. (*Beat; looking out*) It was O K. (*Over shoulder*) You're the funny one. (*He throws open plate glass door, leans against frame, looking out.*)

(*Beat*)

BILLY: Do you miss her? Dad?

DAD: Who?

BILLY: Sharon. I think about her. A whole lot.

(*Beat*)

DAD: Me too.

(*Silence*)

(BILLY *picks up drawing.* DAD *continues looking out.*)

BILLY: Dad?

(*No response*)

BILLY: O K. So. This is the air cleaner. And this is the carburetor. It mixes up the air and gas and then what?

(*No response*)

BILLY: Dad?

DAD: *(Dragging on cigarette; looking out)* It goes down the intake manifold to the combustion chamber.

BILLY: And then what?

DAD: You got spark plugs pokin' in there.

BILLY: In the chamber? Where the gas goes?

(DAD nods, looking out.)

BILLY: And what happens?

(Beat)

DAD: It explodes.

(Lights dim to black.)

(Sound track: the opening bars of Love Is Strange *by Mickey & Sylvia)*

(Lights up. Music continues into:)

Scene Five

(Evening, six months later. Drapes are drawn.)

(BILLY is sitting at table, a book open before him.)

(Enter SHARON in outsized man's shirt and skintight jeans. She is heavily made up. She has two empty beer bottles in her hand.)

(BILLY watches her cross to kitchen. She doesn't look at him.)

(Music fades. As she passes:)

SHARON: So go out.

(SHARON exits into kitchen.)

(BILLY sits, staring at book.)

(Reenter SHARON, with two full beer bottles. Not looking at her brother, she crosses left. As she does so:)

SHARON: You can't get a date? Just this once?

(Exit SHARON *into front room, left.)*

*(*BILLY *continues reading, desultorily.)*

(Reenter SHARON, *empty-handed. She crosses to kitchen, not looking at* BILLY. *To him:)*

SHARON: Go see a movie. *(She exits into kitchen.)*

*(*BILLY *grips the corners of his book.)*

(Reenter SHARON, *with bag of potato chips.)*

SHARON: Or something. *(She crosses left.)*

BILLY: *(Pointing offstage, left)* He gonna stay all night?

SHARON: *(Pausing to look at* BILLY*)* None. Of your business.

BILLY: He gonna play loud music all night?

SHARON: So go in your room at least.

BILLY: They come back tomorrow. Dad'll kill you all this beer and.

(Pause)

SHARON: Billy. Don't be creepoid.

BILLY: What if they come back early?

SHARON: Not from Tahoe. It'll be— *(Gesturing into front room)* All. Cleaned. Up.

BILLY: They'll notice. *(Gesturing off)* He's a slob.

SHARON: From twenty thousand fathoms.

BILLY: Yeah.

SHARON: That's you. The one from twenty thousand fathoms. *(She exits, left.)*

*(*BILLY *slams book shut, rises, exits into kitchen.)*

*(*BILLY *reenters with a carrot. Sits, gnaws)*

(Enter SHARON.)

SHARON: *(Hands on hips)* So?

BILLY: *(Munching)* Huh?

SHARON: So go out. Bobby doesn't like it you're hanging around.

BILLY: He doesn't.

SHARON: No.

(BILLY munches away.)

SHARON: Not one girl. You can't get. One girl.

(BILLY same)

SHARON: Or friends even. Not one friend.

(BILLY same)

SHARON: I thought. You know what I thought? *(Beat)* You woulda changed while I was back east. *(Beat)* But you're just like before. *(Beat)* Grow up, Billy. And go out somewhere.

(Offstage male voice calls: "Sherry!")

BILLY: *(Mimics)* "Sherry."

SHARON: *(Exiting)* Coming, Bobby!

(BILLY gnaws on carrot.)

(Reenter SHARON, crossing into kitchen.)

(She reenters with fresh bottle of beer.)

BILLY: Beer breath all night.

SHARON: Shut up and go to a movie.

BILLY: I ain't got the money.

SHARON: You always got money.

BILLY: Ain't.

SHARON: *(Pointing at him with bottle)* I borrowed. *(Moves closer)* I borrowed five dollars from you and you. Charged me. Interest.

BILLY: So?

SHARON: So don't tell me you don't have it.

BILLY: *(Gesturing off)* Ask beer belly.

(Beat)

SHARON: You. Fucker.

(Exit SHARON, *left.)*

*(*BILLY *stops gnawing, stares at table.)*

(Reenter SHARON; BILLY *abruptly starts munching.)*

SHARON: He's getting mad. *(Beat)* Billy? He'll cream you.

BILLY: I'm so scared. Look at me.

SHARON: *(Placating)* Just for a couple of hours. That's all. Please, Billy.

BILLY: What you gonna do in there? I don't bother you.

SHARON: Don't be stupoid.

BILLY: A pack of Winston.

(Muttering, she exits left.)

*(*BILLY *makes a show of feeling his muscle.)*

*(*SHARON *reenters with a pack of cigarettes. Throws it on table.)*

BILLY: Thanks. I needed a cigarette. *(He lights up, luxuriously puffs.)*

SHARON: You smoke like a dork. *(Beat)* So? Go somewhere.

BILLY: *(Sitting back)* Thanks for the cigarettes.

*(*SHARON *lunges for pack,* BILLY *grabs it, they struggle.)*

(Offstage male voice calls, "Hey Sherry. What's up?")

*(*SHARON *gives up struggle.)*

SHARON: *(Calling off)* It's O K. *(To* BILLY) Liar. Fucker.

BILLY: Dork, huh?

SHARON: The way you smoke. The way you walk.

BILLY: I should smoke like your boyfriend maybe. *(Hunches over, cups hand around cigarette. To her, in gruff voice)* Gimme a beer. *(Huge contempt)* "Sherry."

SHARON: You're not funny anymore. You never were.

BILLY: *(Sprawling in chair)* Hey, baby. *(Fake belch)* I wanna beer. Come on, chick. Gimme a beer. *(Beat; normal voice)* Then I drink it it goes all down my chin and I make you kiss my slimey mouth. *(Resuming normal position in chair)* I'd rather be a dork.

SHARON: That's good. Because you are.

BILLY: Yeah?

SHARON: Yeah.

BILLY: Maybe I should sit around and fart like your boyfriend.

SHARON: He doesn't fart.

BILLY: Then you'd think I was Mister Tough Guy.

SHARON: Tough. You. With your '54 Chevy.

BILLY: *(Bridling)* Shut up.

SHARON: Scag wagon. Queermobile.

BILLY: *(Angry now)* Queer, huh?

SHARON: They say so.

BILLY: Queer, huh?

SHARON: If the shoe fits.

BILLY: *Then how come—?*

(BILLY *and* SHARON *stare at each other.*)

(SHARON *angrily exits, left.*)

(BILLY *sits, staring after her.*)

(BILLY *rises, exits into kitchen.*)

(Reenter BILLY *with beer. He sits, chugalugs it.)*

(Reenter SHARON, *beer in hand. She poses with bottle, biker style, staring at her brother.)*

SHARON: Bobby wants to talk to you.

BILLY: So?

SHARON: Hey. Where'd you get that beer?

BILLY: Kitchen.

SHARON: That's Bobby's beer.

BILLY: Gee.

SHARON: Frip.

BILLY: Who's a frip? He wants to talk to me? He can get off his ass and come in here.

SHARON: Such a tough—

BILLY: Give me no orders.

SHARON: Bunny.

BILLY: I wanna reefer.

(Beat)

SHARON: *(Contemptuously)* You. A reefer.

BILLY: *(Gesturing at front room)* He's the big man at Harvey's Drive-In, he got reefer.

SHARON: So?

BILLY: So tell him.

(Beat)

SHARON: If I get you a reefer. Will you go out somewhere?

BILLY: Sure, chickie.

(SHARON exits into front room. BILLY quickly leans forward, listening.)

(Offstage male voice: "A what?")

(BILLY *snickers and buries his head in book again.*)

(SHARON *reenters;* BILLY *lowers book below eyes.*)

SHARON: *(Holding up J)* This. Is so. Fine. *(Lowers it to his face)* What a waste.

BILLY: *(Staring at J)* Can you die from it?

(Beat, as SHARON *reacts disdainfully)*

BILLY: I mean, if you smoke too much?

(SHARON *stares in contempt; drops J on table. He puts down book, picks up J.*)

BILLY: This. Is it.

SHARON: Light it.

BILLY: *(Examining J)* What end?

SHARON: God. *(She takes J. Gesturing)* This end. Or this end. With a match.

(She starts to light it; He takes J and matches.)

BILLY: You a *real* low-rider? A real low-rider mama?

SHARON: Kissie. Light it. *(Watches as he fumbles with J and matches)* Kissie.

BILLY: *(Puffing)* We'll do like at Harvey's. You be like. My low-rider mama. *(Coughs; blows smoke about)* My chiquita.

(SHARON *grabs J.*)

SHARON: Don't waste it. Like this.

(SHARON *inhales hissingly, holds it, exhales, hands back J.*)

BILLY: I get you. *(He inhales, holds it. Gasping:)* How long. I gotta. Hold it?

SHARON: *(Sitting; exasperated)* Fudd.

BILLY: *(Same)* How long?

(SHARON *sits, waiting.*)

(BILLY *exhales coughingly. Beat*)

BILLY: I don't feel nothin.

SHARON: Farmer. Take some more.

(*Again he inhales, hissingly.*)

SHARON: You're gonna get sick.

(*Again* BILLY *exhales, coughing.*)

(SHARON *giggles.*)

BILLY: (*Sprawling in chair; indicating J*) This ain't so tough.

SHARON: Goody gumdrops. With a reefer.

BILLY: I'm as bad as anybody.

SHARON: Yeah? (*She takes J, inhales, hands it back.*) So why don't you go out. To like Harvey's? And prove it.

BILLY: Maybe I will.

SHARON: (*Contemptuously*) In your '54 Chevy.

BILLY: (*Into her face*) Maybe I'll pick up a slut!

(*Beat*)

(*Angrily,* SHARON *plucks J from* BILLY'*s fingers. Rises, stands over him, J in her mouth, hand on her hip, biker-style, defiant and provocative.*)

SHARON: Maybe she'll laugh at you.

(BILLY *also stands, taking J from* SHARON'*s lips.*)

BILLY: Maybe she won't.

(BILLY *and* SHARON *are nose to nose.*)

SHARON: She'd laugh at your dorkie clothes.

BILLY: (*Mimics Bobby*) Come on, chick. Gimme some.

SHARON: At your dorkie glasses.

BILLY: Gimme gimme.

SHARON: At your dorkie car.

BILLY: Shut up!

SHARON: At your creepy walk and your fairy talk and your—

BILLY: *Gimme!*

(Violently, BILLY *embraces* SHARON, *crushing his mouth against hers. She struggles.)*

SHARON: Stop it!

(Offstage male voice: "Sherry?")

*(*BILLY *and* SHARON *break; she crosses in direction of front room.)*

SHARON: *(Angrily calling off)* Just a minute! *(She slowly crosses back to* BILLY.*)*

*(*SHARON *spits in* BILLY'*s face.)*

*(*BILLY *closes his eyes; otherwise does not react.)*

(Offstage male voice: "Sherry! What the hell?")

SHARON: *(Still staring at her brother)* Coming, Bobby. *(Beat)* Want another beer? Bobby? *(Beat)* Whatever you want, Bobby. Just ask.

*(*BILLY *discards J on table, marches out of room.)*

SHARON: *(To herself; triumphant)* Whatever. You. Want.

(Blackout)

(Sound track: the opening bars of Daddy's Home *by Shep & the Limelights)*

(Music fades. Lights up on:)

Scene Six

(Dinnertime, three months later. Drapes open. DAD *and* MOM *sit glumly at table, on which is a whiskey bottle, glasses, and a bowl of corn chips, dry and crackling, from which they periodically eat.)*

(Silence. Then:)

DAD: Christ almighty god. *(He drinks.)*

MOM: I know.

DAD: *(Louder)* Christ Jesus.

MOM: Well, we raised her. *(She drinks, makes a face.)*

DAD: Don't gimme that. That crap we raised her.

MOM: I know.

(Beat)

DAD: This time. The guy marries her.

MOM: I suppose.

DAD: She out with him?

MOM: They went to Harvey's.

DAD: *(Huge contempt)* Harvey's.

MOM: Doesn't matter now. Where she goes.

DAD: What's he do?

MOM: Drop out. Seven-eleven.

DAD: You mean like that liquor store?

MOM: *(Drinking, with a shrug)* Beer and wine. Says he guesses. He'll marry her.

DAD: Jesus H Christ. Seven-eleven. She was going to *airline* school!

MOM: Billy can go to college.

DAD: Some stumblebum offa Seven-eleven. Jesus H Almighty God. She won't even graduate high school.

MOM: Oh well. I guess they'd let her. If she weren't—

DAD: *(Bitterly; refilling glass)* Knocked up again.

MOM: Anyway. I guess he'll marry her. Says he will. Strangest thing.

DAD: What's so strange a stumblebum?

MOM: He reminds me of guys during. The war. Girls too. Nobody cared. Just. Get married.

DAD: What are you? We cared. We knew what we were doing.

MOM: Honey. We got married. Fast.

DAD: So? It was different then. Anyways. A guy coulda died. And we loved each other. That's the difference. She can't love that.

MOM: She doesn't. She told me so.

(Beat)

DAD: You mean. She's not gonna go through with it?

MOM: No. She knows she's got to this time.

DAD: *(Relieved)* My little girl. To a cashier. At a liquor-eleven. We didn't raise her for this.

MOM: We raised her.

DAD: Would you cut out this we raised her crap? Look at me. My stepdad in Chicago. Threw me out I was fourteen years old. Middle the Depression. Did I go out and mess around? At Harvey's?

MOM: It's harder for a girl.

DAD: I never had a chance go to airline college. *(Bangs table)* She spits on us!

(Beat; DAD drinks.)

MOM: Billy can go to college.

DAD: *(Frowning as he drinks)* Billy.

MOM: He's O K.

DAD: Something. I dunno. Wrong there.

MOM: Honey? He's all right.

DAD: Sharon was my little girl. Remember I usta drive with her in my lap? She was just a button but she'd put her little hands on the wheel and play like she was drivin'. We'd go faster and faster and faster and faster. She couldn't get enough and she loved it. *Laugh?* Boy, could she laugh. *(Drinks)* It was right after they put in the Santa Ana. Jesus.

MOM: Billy's never been in trouble.

DAD: You grew up that old bastard out in Riverside that apricot farm? Wouldn't even let you go to a dance. You whoored around? No. Never. *(Drinks) Jesus.*

MOM: *(Drinking also)* There's nothing wrong with Billy.

DAD: I dunno.

MOM: He's O K.

DAD: Somethin'. Funny.

MOM: Don't make a federal case. *(Rising)* You want supper? I could make. A meat loaf.

DAD: *(Shakes head; pouring)* Drink up.

(MOM sits. They drink.)

DAD: What makes her do these things? Sweetie? What?

MOM: It's like they don't care.

DAD: *(Exploding) What you mean they don't care!* *(Mimics wildly)* "They don't care!" "They don't care!" *(Beat)* Now. I asked you a question.

MOM: *(Drinking)* I don't know.

DAD: Why don't you know?

MOM: Stop it.

DAD: I. Asked you. A question.

MOM: She did it. To hurt. *(Beat; not looking at* DAD*)* Us.

DAD: *Crap! (Beat)* She was my little girl.

MOM: Honey. She hasn't been your little girl. In a long time.

DAD: I was in Germany. So goddamned wet and with filth. I get your letter and I can't stop tellin' the guys. I said I wanted a boy. Gotta have a boy.

MOM: You were tickled pink when you saw her.

DAD: Oh, man. She was so cute. I wanted. To gobble her up, *(Beat; quickly)* What's wrong with that?

MOM: I didn't say it was—

DAD: I loved her! Right down here in my guts I loved her. *(Bitterly)* Hurt us. *(Beat)* Crap. It was when she got tits.

MOM: *(Shaking her head)* Oh, honey.

DAD: Twelve was awful young for tits that big.

MOM: It wasn't that.

DAD: It was that.

MOM: No.

DAD: It makes sense! *(Mimics again)* "They don't care!" "Hurt us!" That makes. No. Sense. If you're gonna talk to me. Make. Sense. *(Beat)* You hear me?

MOM: *(Rising)* I better get supper.

DAD: *Sit down! (Beat)* And talk to me.

*(*MOM *sits.)*

DAD: She just go outa here and said. You tell Dad? And left with this stumblebum for. Harvey's?

MOM: I guess so.

DAD: That place. Is like a Marineland of Mexican. Or white grease oughta be Mexican. Drive around and around the parking lot what kinna fun is that? *(Beat)* *We* went to the Hollywood Palladium.

MOM: *(Drinking)* I cried.

DAD: You what?

MOM: When Glen Miller got killed. I cried.

DAD: Sure. The big bands. We was lucky to find somebody hadda car. We didn't drive around and around. *(Beat)* And around and around. *(Beat)* And around and around and around. *(He bangs table.)*

MOM: Honey. I told her she could go. Said *I'd* tell you. Don't worry, I said. Just go.

DAD: You told her that.

MOM: And I gave Billy some money for gas. He won't go to Harvey's. I just wanted us. To be alone here.

DAD: Alone here.

MOM: It's best. *(Beat)* Billy'll go. To Hollywood.

DAD: *(Contemptuous)* Hollywood.

MOM: The bookstores.

DAD: *(Drinking)* Hollywood is not. What it was. We hadda job out to Westwood just this twelve-inch it was a piece of cake. So anyways. We seen this pansy on Hollywood Boulevard. Walkin' a *poodle.*

MOM: Honey. He goes to the bookstores.

DAD: Faggots go to bookstores! Who you think buys all those books?

(Beat; DAD and MOM are distinctly drunk.)

MOM: It's wrong. What we're doing. *(Hands to her face)* She shouldn't. Marry him.

DAD: Nobody give me a car. I was in the eighth grade my stepdad says. Get out. With this *crowbar* in his hand. Just like that. Puts me on the street with a crowbar.

MOM: *(Looking up; suddenly angry)* Your mother.

DAD: Middle the Depression.

MOM: *(Same)* Your mother. How could she just stand by? Let that old. Son of a.

(Overlapping:)

DAD: Ended up on the goddamn federal works.

MOM: *(Making fists)* She was so self-righteous about Sharon. So pure. So *religious.*

DAD: Nobody gave me a goddamn. Four in the morning.

MOM: And she just.

DAD: I'd get up. Four in the morning. Winter and summer.

MOM: She didn't love you.

(Beat)

DAD: Who didn't?

MOM: Your mother.

DAD: My mother?

MOM: All that about her sacrifices. And she stood there while that son of a gun put you on the street. To starve.

DAD: She couldn't help it.

MOM: Oh, no. Couldn't help it.

(Overlapping:)

DAD: It's still dark at four in the morning.

MOM: Just stood there. Watching. If *you* tried that.

DAD: Winter mornings back east? You can't see your hand it's so dark.

MOM: If you tried that with Billy.

DAD: And they turn into whoors. Right in your face.

MOM: I'd stop you. I swear it.

DAD: Weekends those kids sleep 'til noon!

MOM: I'd stop you or I'd. Go with him.

DAD: Sashayin' down Hollywood Boulevard.

MOM: It's got. To stop.

DAD: Or some taco wagon at Harvey's—well, this time she *marries* the taco wagon!

MOM: *(Exploding) It's got to stop!*

(Silence)

(MOM sits, head in hands. DAD looks away. Drinks)

DAD: You better get supper.

MOM: *(Head still in hands)* Scrambled eggs. I could scramble some eggs.

DAD: Sure.

MOM: *(Dropping hands)* With onions.

(Beat)

DAD: Sweetie. I'm tired.

MOM: Hard. *(Beat; looking at him)* Day?

DAD: La Puente. Hell and gone.

MOM: *(Rising)* Honey?

DAD: Yeah?

MOM: You always. Put the food on the table. *(Touches his shoulder tenderly; a wan smile)* And you never ran around on me.

(DAD covers MOM's hand with his.)

(They stare at table.)

(Lights dim to black.)

(Sound track: the opening bars of Come On, Let's Go *by Richie Valens)*

(Lights up. Music continues into:)

Scene Seven

(Morning, two weeks later. The drapes are opened, and the brilliant California sunshine pours in through the plate glass, gilding the room. A small wedding cake and plastic flower arrangement on the table. A plate of finger sandwiches and napkins.)

*(*BILLY *is standing and looking out onto patio, snapping his fingers to the music. He is dressed in flecked sports jacket and slacks.)*

*(*SHARON, *seated at table, is dressed in cream-colored tailored suit and tiara, looking into a compact and fussing with her hair and makeup.)*

(Music out. BILLY *moves into room, sits at table.)*

BILLY: *(Taking out cigarette)* Hey, chickie. You look good.

SHARON: *(Into compact)* I know.

BILLY: *Real* good.

SHARON: Thanks.

BILLY: I mean. Like a model.

*(*SHARON *notices* BILLY *is lighting up.)*

SHARON: Better not, Billy. Mom and Dad only went out for liquor. They won't like it they catch you smoking.

*(*BILLY *shrugs, lights up. Exhales)*

BILLY: So when we gotta be there?

SHARON: By noon.

BILLY: Why there? In that church? We ain't religious.

SHARON: Bobby's parents.

BILLY: They're weird.

SHARON: You can put up with them this once. It's just us. And them. *(Snapping compact shut; ironically:)* It's a quiet affair.

BILLY: Their house is weird. Okieville.

SHARON: Daddy likes them O K.

BILLY: No, he don't. And Mom don't either. Okies.

SHARON: So? Mom's people were Tennessee.

BILLY: But Mom was *born* in California. She's first generation.

SHARON: Big deal.

BILLY: Mom says. Bobby's folks are white trash. *(Laughs)* And Dad says yeah but anyways they're white.

SHARON: *(Also laughing; in spite of herself)* He's. Something. He really thought. I'd marry a Negro.

BILLY: All that Johnny Otis on T V. *(Snapping fingers; sings:)* "De bop bama looma, de bop bam boom!"

SHARON: Daddy's such a. *(Stops laughing)* Jerk.

BILLY: Yeah. *(Beat)* He thinks I'm queer.

(SHARON looks away.)

SHARON: I just wanna. Get this over with.

BILLY: So you guys gonna live here? Or in Bell Gardens?

SHARON: With Bobby's folks? No way.

BILLY: God. That refrigerator torn apart on the front lawn? God, That car torn apart in the driveway? God. They just cut the grass around the spare parts.

SHARON: *When* they cut the grass. No. Way.

BILLY: So here?

SHARON: Daddy's giving us. Some money for an apartment. In Norwalk.

BILLY: Norwalk's Mexican!

SHARON: Only until. The baby comes. Then I guess. Someplace.

BILLY: The baby.

SHARON: *(Laughing)* You're not supposed to know.

BILLY: I can figure it out.

SHARON: I dunno. So can everybody else. *(Looks at table)* This is stupid.

BILLY: Even the cake is sad.

(Beat)

SHARON: *(Checking watch)* Where are they?

BILLY: Prob'ly bought some liquor then stopped off for a drink. They been drinkin' like fishoids.

SHARON: Guess what?

BILLY: What?

SHARON: Dad said. I didn't have to go through with it.

BILLY: When?

SHARON: The other night. Can you believe it?

BILLY: He didn't mean it.

SHARON: I know. But wasn't that—?

BILLY: Oh sure. And what? Send you back east to Grandma's? Do it all over again?

SHARON: Shut up! *(Beat)* That. Didn't happen.

BILLY: Crapola.

(Beat. BILLY *begins tasting frosting of cake with his fingertip.)*

SHARON: Stop that.

*(*BILLY *continues.)*

SHARON: Billy!

BILLY: *(Tasting)* It's gooey.

SHARON: Leave it. Alone.

BILLY: It's funny. Just sitting there. All squatty. And these dippy little sandwiches!

SHARON: They're supposed to be *elegant.*

BILLY: *(Shaking head over food)* Mom sure hates to cook.

SHARON: *(Giggling)* Yeah. Look at that cake.

BILLY: She shoulda put onions in it.

SHARON: A liver wedding cake!

*(*BILLY *and* SHARON *bust up giggling.)*

BILLY: Hey. Look at me. *(Makes a heavy moronic face)*

SHARON: What are you doing?

BILLY: I'm Bobby. *(Points at sandwiches; holds one up)* And this. Is you. Watch. *(Shoves it into his mouth. Eats grossly as his sister stares)*

SHARON: *Stop it!*

*(*SHARON *rises, looking away.* BILLY *ceases moronic eating, wipes mouth.)*

SHARON: God, everybody's right. You're such a—

BILLY: *(Cutting her off)* Know what I think?

SHARON: Who cares?

BILLY: I think we shoulda gone away. To like. Seal Beach. I coulda learned to surf. We coulda raised it.

SHARON: Are you. Crazy?

BILLY: Or Hollywood. They never woulda found us in Hollywood.

(SHARON *begins laughing; sits; between giggles:*)

SHARON: Kids at school. Think you're. But you're not. Know what you are? You're a *loon!*

BILLY: Maybe I am. Queer.

(SHARON *stops laughing.*)

BILLY: Everybody says so. So maybe I am.

SHARON: It's just the way you. Act.

BILLY: But if everybody says it. Maybe I should be it. Dad don't say it. But he thinks it.

SHARON: That's not. True.

BILLY: But if everybody wants me to be queer, then maybe I should be! I mean. (*Shakes head*) God.

SHARON: (*Softly*) Don't. Let them.

BILLY: Don't let them what?

SHARON: Make you queer.

BILLY: Oh? Like they're making you. (*Points at cake*) Do this?

SHARON: Be quiet.

BILLY: (*Eagerly*) We could run away. Right now. We should raise this one like we shoulda raised the other one!

SHARON: (*Rising from chair*) Shut up! (*Beat; fidgeting*) This is Bobby's baby I'm gonna be Bobby's wife; you're crazy.

BILLY: The other one was mine!

SHARON: *Forget that!* That didn't. Happen. That should never—

BILLY: Dennis. It wasn't no Dennis.

SHARON: *(Jabbing finger at him)* Don't you say this to Bobby. Don't you. *Ever*. Mention this to. *Anybody*.

BILLY: Dennis was a hot air. Just like Bobby.

SHARON: What did I just say?

BILLY: *(Stubbornly)* The other one was mine.

SHARON: It was. Not.

BILLY: You said so!

SHARON: Because I wanted— *(Beat; sadly)* To hurt you. *(She fidgets with flower arrangements.)*

BILLY: Oh. Thanks a lot.

SHARON: *(Mimics)* "Thanks a lot." Shit. *(Beat)* I had to. Take it all. You would just sit here and nothing—

BILLY: Bull.

SHARON: Ever happened to you.

BILLY: Yeah? So what about that time he makes me go into Little League?

SHARON: *It's not the same! (Beat; disdainfully:)* Little League. God.

BILLY: Dad said he was gonna Scotch Tape my mitt to my hand.

SHARON: *(Laughing)* You sure looked funnoid in that uniform.

BILLY: Not as funny as Dad. When he usta walk around naked in front of us?

SHARON: *(Uneasily; moving to plate glass)* Billy.

BILLY: Remember? Always said. Take a gander.
(Rises, imitates fowl) "Take a gander! Take a gander!"
(Laughing) What's that, like a goose?

(SHARON laughs, remembering.)

SHARON: That pot belly!

BILLY: Those knobby knees!

SHARON: God!

BILLY: Come on, let's do the Gander Stomp!

SHARON: Do the Stewardess Stomp!

(Using arms and elbows as wings, they stomp about, laughing.)

(Suddenly, BILLY grabs SHARON.)

BILLY: Sharon, it wasn't no Dennis!

(SHARON breaks away from BILLY.)

SHARON: It was so!

(SHARON returns to plate glass, looks out. BILLY sits.)

(Beat)

BILLY: *(Disdainfully)* Dennis.

(SHARON is silent, indifferent, looking out at backyard.)

BILLY: Said he used a rubber.

(SHARON freezes.)

BILLY: Dennis told it all over school how he used one.

SHARON: *(Not looking at him)* He. What?

BILLY: Said he took *precaution*. Such a big man. I knew
he was full of it.

(Beat, as SHARON continues staring out)

SHARON: He *was*. Full of it. *(Turns, looks at BILLY)* You
all are.

BILLY: It was mine!

SHARON: *So! Fucking! What? (Beat. She sits.)* You're supposed to be. Happy. On your wedding day. But I feel. Like. I have to catch a bus.

BILLY: Like the first day of the school year. All queasy.

SHARON: Uh-huh. Like it's gonna be a long time.

BILLY: Until summer.

SHARON: Yeah.

(BILLY *and* SHARON *stare at cake.*)

BILLY: I'm a queer and you're a slut. So we should. Go away.

SHARON: *(Rising)* Go to hell.

BILLY: It was my baby. And you let them—

SHARON: *Let* them?

BILLY: Give it away.

SHARON: Oh. Right. I shoulda given it to you. Oh. I see. And you coulda. Dressed it up. In little frillies? And played with it.

BILLY: Shut up.

SHARON: Billy. You had nothing to do with that. Guys don't. You're just. Things.

BILLY: *I* was?

SHARON: *(Offhand; cynical)* Sure. Guys are just things. Licking. And biting. Then they marry you and you live in Norwalk.

BILLY: I. Was this *thing* to you?

SHARON: *(Same)* Sure. 1 didn't feel anything. I never feel anything. *(Beat)*

(BILLY *slowly rises and picks a plastic flower out of arrangement.*)

BILLY: A thing. Like this?

(BILLY *tosses flower at* SHARON; *no reaction*)

BILLY: A rubbery. (*Picks another*) Fake. (*Throws flower violently into her face*) Thing!

(SHARON *turns away, rubbing her cheek.* BILLY *sits, stares at floor.*)

SHARON: Billy. I'm really sorry. About all. That. So just forget it, O K?

BILLY: (*Mimics*) "Just forget it, O K?"

SHARON: (*Looks at watch*) They did stop for a drink. (*Looking at table*) We better put the flowers back. (*Laughing*) For the *reception*. (*She picks up plastic flowers from floor, then all at once twirls, girlishly, irrepressibly, then replaces flowers. Fussing:*) You'll get married someday.

BILLY: Queers don't get married.

SHARON: Oh, Billy. (*She sits down again, crosses her hands in her lap, demurely:*) You will. Someday.

(BILLY *makes a flatulent noise with his lips.*)

SHARON: (*Smiling*) You're just a kid.

BILLY: Oh, hey. (*Rises*) Here we got. (*Gesturing*) The old married lady.

SHARON: (*Self-deprecating*) I know.

BILLY: God. You're two years older than me. This is not. A long time.

SHARON: (*Same*) I know.

BILLY: So don't gimme that. Mature crapoid.

SHARON: It changes you. That's all.

BILLY: *I'm* still the same.

SHARON: I meant. Marriage.

BILLY: Oh. You mean. *(Circles table, pointing at cake)* This does? *(Beat)* This sad. Ugly. *(He sinks his hand into cake.)* Thing?

(SHARON stares.)

(Silence)

(She looks away.)

SHARON: Oh well.

(BILLY withdraws hand, looks at it.)

BILLY: *(Extending hand towards her)* Want some?

SHARON: Daddy'll. Kill you.

BILLY: *(Same)* Want some? *(Beat)* Go ahead. *(He thrusts his begooed hand close to her averted face.)* Lick it off my fingers. *(Beat, as slowly she looks at his hand)* Go ahead. *(Thrusts hand)* Lick it!

(Pause)

(SHARON calmly looks from BILLY's hand to his face.)

SHARON: You can't.

BILLY: Can't what?

SHARON: *(Shrugging)* Do that. *(Looking away)* I don't live here anymore.

(Slowly BILLY withdraws hand. He seems confused as he looks about at random.)

(Finally, he flicks goo from his hand back into cake.)

BILLY: God. I messed it. Bad.

SHARON: I'll say it was me. That I'm just. I dunno. Nervous.

BILLY: Will you? Sharon?

SHARON: *(Nodding)* Something.

(Meekly, BILLY takes napkin, wipes his hand, sits down again.)

(Silence. They stare at floor.)

(All at once SHARON *impishly begins humming, then singing, the opening bars to the song* "Speedo".*)*

SHARON: "Well now they often call me Speedo—" *(She looks at him.)*

BILLY: *(Picking it up)* "But my real name is—" *(He taps shoe in time. Chiming:)*

BILLY & SHARON: *(In unison)* "Mister Earl."

(They laugh and repeat refrain, SHARON *snapping her fingers.* BILLY *trails off as* SHARON *continues singing.)*

BILLY: *(Under her singing)* Sharon?

*(*SHARON *continues singing.)*

BILLY: Was it. A boy?

(She abruptly falls silent.)

BILLY: Or a girl?

SHARON: *(Shrugging)* A boy, I think.

(Beat)

BILLY: Was he. O K?

SHARON: I dunno.

BILLY: You don't. Know?

SHARON: I didn't see him.

BILLY: Didn't even. See him?

SHARON: He wasn't very strong, I think.

BILLY: He wasn't—

(Beat)

SHARON: *(Dropping eyes)* Very strong.

(Sound track: Speedo *by the Cadillacs. Lights dim.)*

END OF PLAY

www.ingramcontent.com/pod-product-compliance
Lightning Source LLC
Chambersburg PA
CBHW052211090426
42741CB00010B/2501